Spot it!®

Puzzle Book

Special thanks to Michaël Goncalves, Maxime Jegat, Sébastien Milloux, Stéphanie Berri, Priscillia Dubois, Olivier Delattre, and Thomas Dussud with Zygomatic Studio, and to Danielle Robb at Asmodee Entertainment.

Published in 2022 by Welbeck
an imprint of Welbeck Non-Fiction,
part of Welbeck Publishing Group
Based in London and Sydney
www.welbeckpublishing.com

Puzzles and Design © 2022 Welbeck Non-Fiction Ltd,
part of Welbeck Publishing Group

Editorial and Design: Tall Tree Limited
Design Manager: Eliana Holder
Production Controller: Marion Storz

A CIP catalogue for this book is available from the British Library.

ISBN: 978-1-80279-103-7

Printed in China

10 9 8 7 6 5 4 3 2 1

Published by Welbeck Non-Fiction Ltd under a license from Asmodee Group. All rights reserved. Spot It! is a game by Denis Blanchot, Jacques Cottereau and the Play Factory Company. Spot it!, Dobble, and Dobble characters are trademarks of Asmodee Group.

Spot it®!

Puzzle Book

ENTERTAINING VISUAL PUZZLES BASED
ON THE CLASSIC SPOT IT! SYMBOLS

JASON WARD

WELBECK

Introduction

Every time you play Spot It!, it feels a little bit like a magic trick. You look at the card in your hand and somehow it holds precisely one symbol that matches the card on the table. Meanwhile, the card on the table also holds a different symbol that matches the card in your opponent's hand. How is that even possible?

You only have seconds to ponder this notion, however, because then the other player yells "SUNGLASSES!" and you've lost. But only for a moment: there's always another card, another mysterious, mind-bending quirk of the symbols, another chance at Spot It! glory!

SPOT THE MATCH!

This book aims to conjure the thrill of playing Spot It! by forcing your brain to make ingenious leaps. To recreate that moment when you've been staring at two cards, seemingly forever, half-convinced that nothing matches at all, until suddenly—there it is!—you've spotted a waving hand with jaunty little legs. As well as the opportunity to go head-to-head against a friend in classic Spot It! fashion, you'll find an array of visual puzzles to tax your powers of observation and speed.

The answer is always there... sometimes you just need to squint for a bit.

Seeing Double

Which Spot It! symbol appears only once in this jumble?

# Iconography

Divide these symbols into sections by drawing lines so that each section contains one of each symbol.

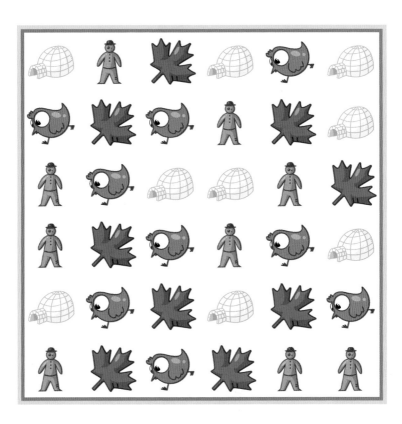

A Lost Piece

Which of the fragments below fit into the missing spaces?

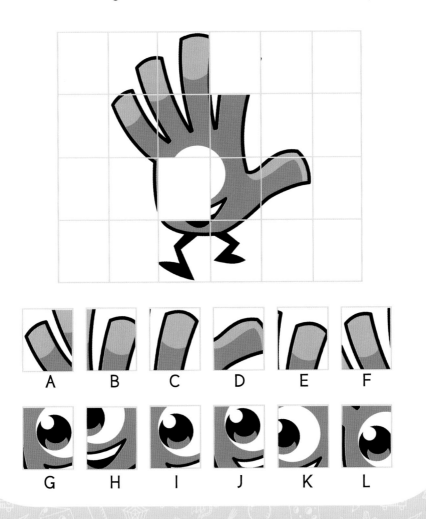

A   B   C   D   E   F

G   H   I   J   K   L

Make a Loop:
a game for 2 players

PLAYER 1

Start and finish here

8

How to play:

Lay the book between the two players so that both can see their own page. In classic Spot It! style, you progress by finding the identical symbol between a card and the next one along the trail. The winner of this head-to-head contest is the first player to make a complete loop back to their starting card.

Ready? On your marks, get set... GO!

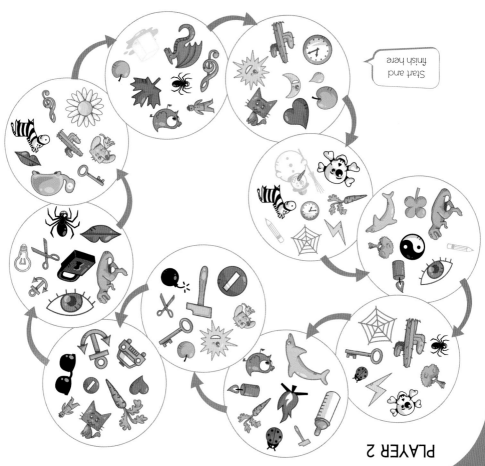

Start and finish here

PLAYER 2

9

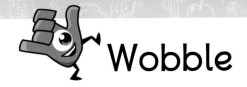

Wobble

Which square is wrong, and why?

Spot (It!) the Difference

Spot the six differences between these two Spot It! cards.

Shady Business

Which of these silhouettes is an accurate
reflection of the Spot It! mascot?

A

B

C

D

E

F

Find the Pair

Which Spot It! symbol appears twice in this jumble?

Odd One Out

Which Spot It! symbol is the odd one out?

Mirrors

Which two collections of Spot It! symbols are exact mirror images?

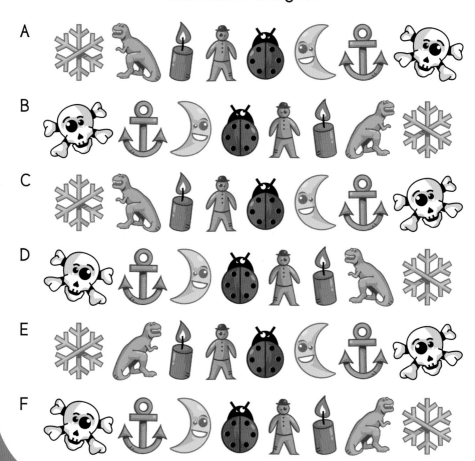

Off the Grid

Put these Spot It! symbols back together by entering the correct grid references in the blank grid as shown below.

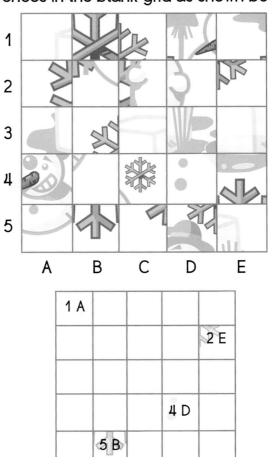

1 A				
				2 E
			4 D	
	5 B			

 # Spot It!

Add a horizontal, vertical or diagonal arrow to each empty square. The symbols indicate how many arrows should be pointing to them and each arrow can point to more than one symbol.

 2 arrows

 3 arrows

 4 arrows

 5 arrows

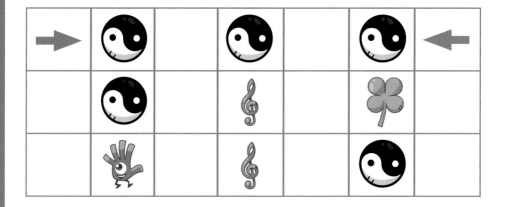

Seeing Double

Which Spot It! symbol appears only once in this jumble?

Make a Loop:
a game for 2 players

PLAYER 1

Start and finish here

18

How to play:

Lay the book between the two players so that both can see their own page. In classic Spot It! style, you progress by finding the identical symbol between a card and the next one along the trail. The winner of this head-to-head contest is the first player to make a complete loop back to their starting card.

Ready? On your marks, get set... GO!

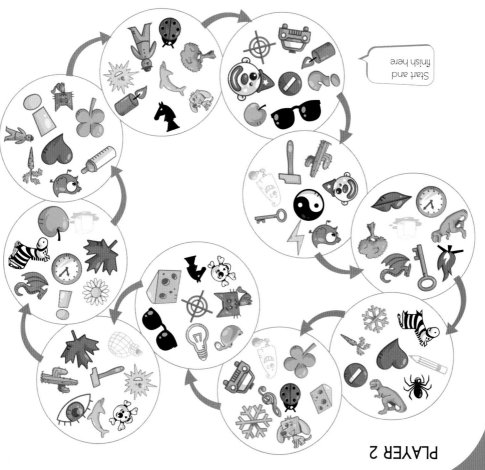

Start and finish here

PLAYER 2

19

Spot (It!) the Difference

Spot the six differences between these two Spot It! cards.

 A Trespasser

Find the intruder among these Spot It! symbols.

Iconography

Divide these symbols into sections by drawing lines so that each section contains one of each symbol.

Shady Business

Which of these silhouettes is an accurate reflection of this scene?

A

B

C

D

E

F

Odd One Out

Which Spot It! symbol is the odd one out?

Find the Pair

Which Spot It! symbol appears twice in this jumble?

Follow That Hand!

Create a loop that passes through every symbol.

The loop doesn't have to turn in a square, but if it does then it can only move in the direction indicated by the symbol: The Spot It! symbol means up, the Dinosaur means left, the Dragon means right, the Spider means down, and the Target means any direction. It must not enter the empty yellow square.

Mirrors

Which two collections of Spot It! symbols are exact mirror images?

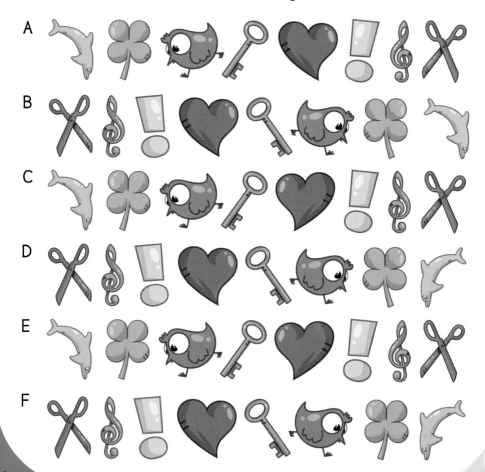

Wobble

There are four unusual squares. Which of these squares is wrong, and why?

 A Trespasser

Find the intruder among these Spot It! symbols.

Make a Loop:
a game for 2 players

PLAYER 1

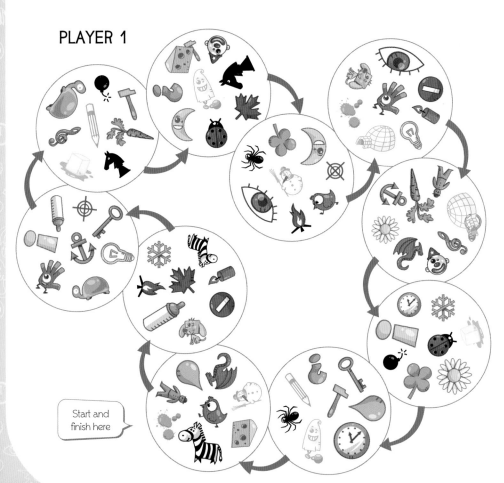

Start and
finish here

How to play:

Lay the book between the two players so that both can see their own page. In classic Spot It! style, you progress by finding the identical symbol between a card and the next one along the trail. The winner of this head-to-head contest is the first player to make a complete loop back to their starting card.

Ready? On your marks, get set... GO!

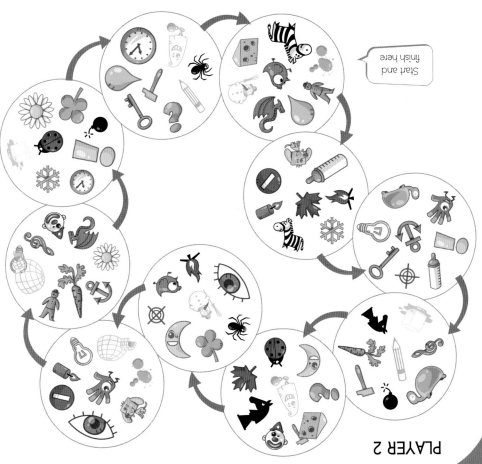

Start and finish here

PLAYER 2

Off the Grid

Unscramble these Spot It! symbols and enter the correct grid references in the blank grid, as shown below.

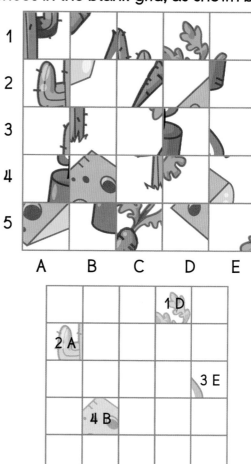

			1 D	
2 A				
				3 E
	4 B			

Spot It!

Add a horizontal, vertical, or diagonal arrow to each empty square. The symbols indicate how many arrows should be pointing to them and each arrow can point to more than one symbol.

 1 arrow

 2 arrows

 3 arrows

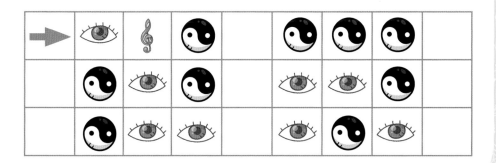

A Lost Piece

Which of the fragments below fit into the missing spaces?

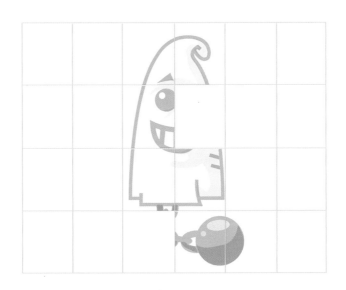

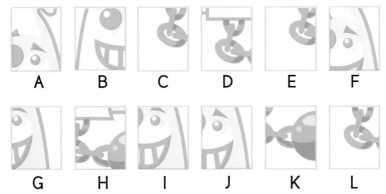

A   B   C   D   E   F

G   H   I   J   K   L

Seeing Double

Which Spot It! symbol appears only once in this jumble?

Odd One Out

Which Spot It! symbol is the odd one out?

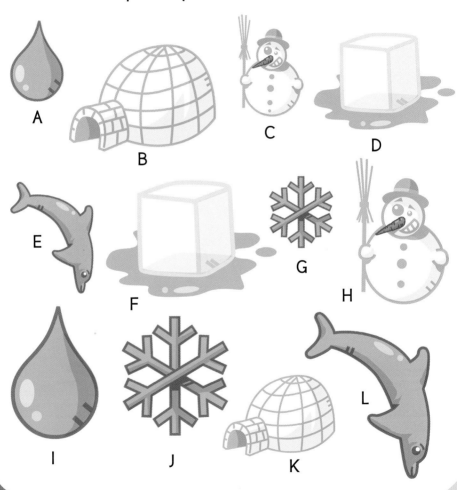

Iconography

Divide these symbols into sections by drawing lines so that each section contains one of each symbol.

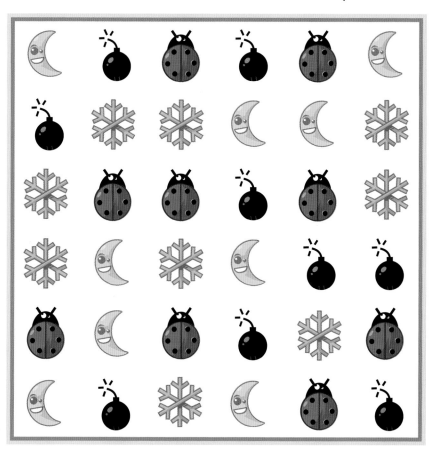

Shady Business

Which of these silhouettes is an accurate reflection of the Snowman symbol?

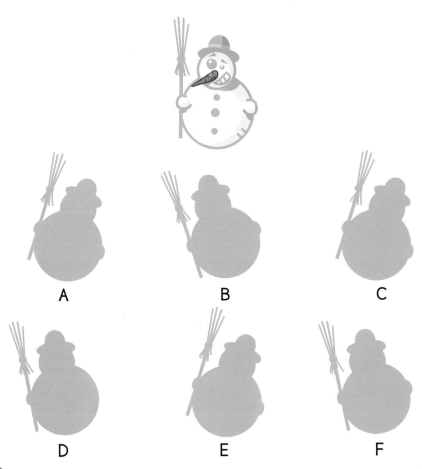

A

B

C

D

E

F

Mirrors

Which two collections of Spot It! symbols are exact mirror images?

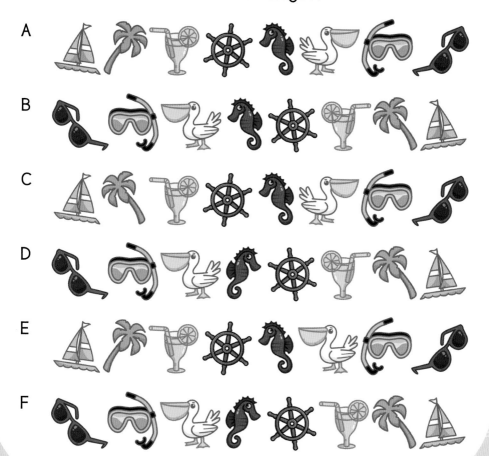

A

B

C

D

E

F

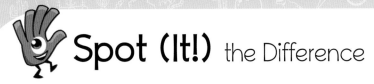

Spot (It!) the Difference

Spot the six differences between these two Spot It! cards.

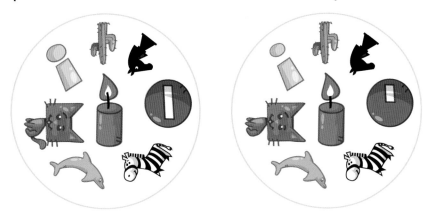

Summer Sums

$$\text{sunglasses} + \text{flower} + \text{sunglasses} = 75$$

$$1 \times \text{flower} = \text{sunglasses}$$

$$\text{sun} \times \text{sun} = 64$$

What are each of the three symbols worth?

Find the Pair

Which Spot It! symbol appears twice in this jumble?

Make a Loop:
a game for 2 players

PLAYER 1

Start and finish here

40

How to play:

Lay the book between the two players so that both can see their own page. In classic Spot It! style, you progress by finding the identical symbol between a card and the next one along the trail. The winner of this head-to-head contest is the first player to make a complete loop back to their starting card.

Ready? On your marks, get set... GO!

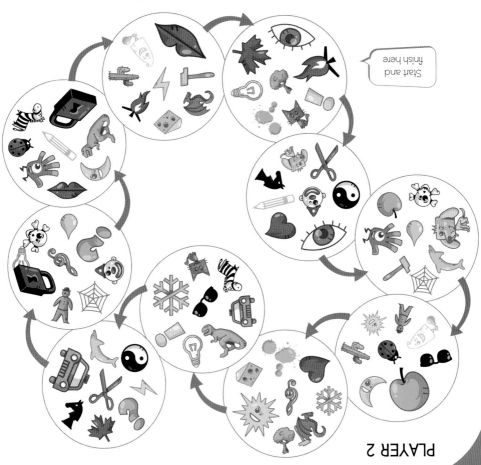

Start and finish here

PLAYER 2

41

# Dividing Lines

Add three straight lines dividing the box below so that each Dragon is in its own section.

Off the Grid

Put these Spot It! symbols back together by entering the correct grid references in the blank grid, as shown below.

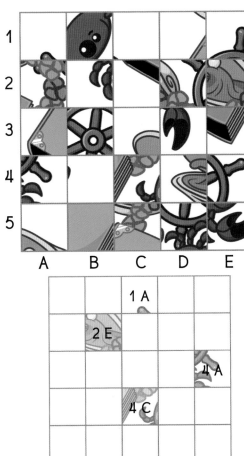

Odd One Out

Which Spot It! symbol is the odd one out?

A

B

C

D

E

F

G

H

Seeing Double

Which Spot It! symbol appears only once in this jumble?

Follow That Hand!

Create a loop that passes through every symbol.

The loop doesn't have to turn in a square, but if it does then it can only move in the direction indicated by the symbol: the Spot It! symbol means up, the Dinosaur means left, the Dragon means right, and the Spider means down.

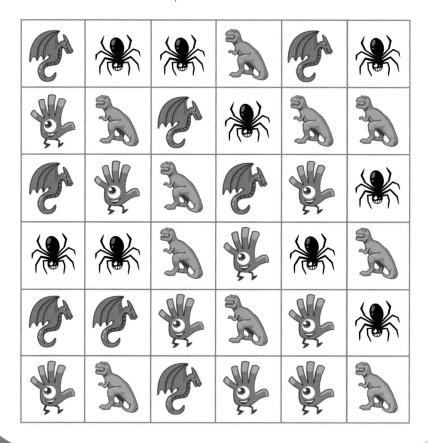

Iconography

Divide these symbols into sections so that every region contains exactly one of each symbol.

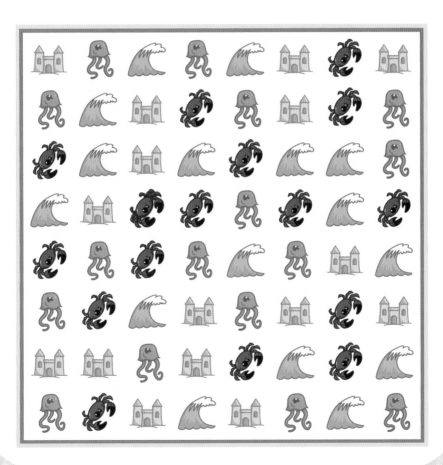

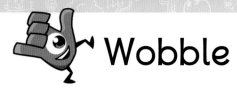 # Wobble

Which square doesn't follow the same logic
as the other squares, and why?

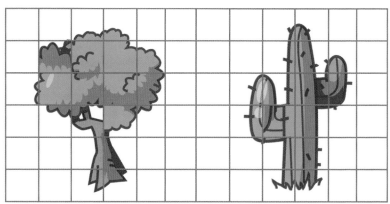

Spot (It!) the Difference

Spot the six differences between these two Spot It! cards.

Mirrors

Which two collections of Spot It! symbols are exact mirror images?

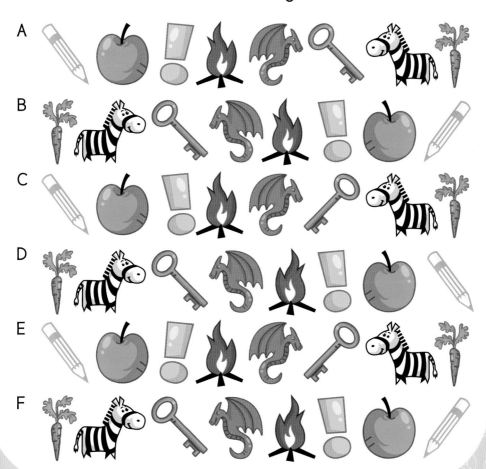

A

B

C

D

E

F

Make a Loop:
a game for 2 players

PLAYER 1

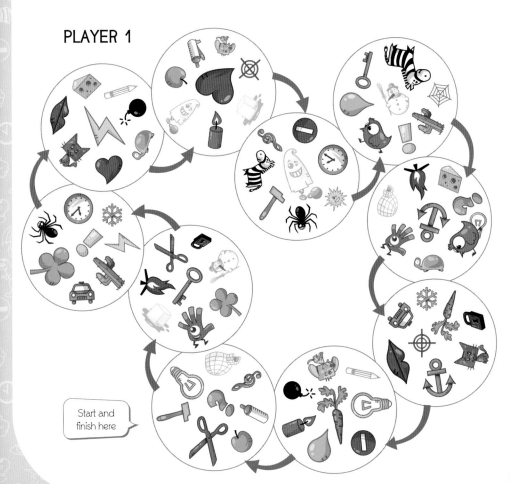

Start and
finish here

50

How to play:

Lay the book between the two players so that both can see their own page. In classic Spot It! style, you progress by finding the identical symbol between a card and the next one along the trail. The winner of this head-to-head contest is the first player to make a complete loop back to their starting card.

Ready? On your marks, get set... GO!

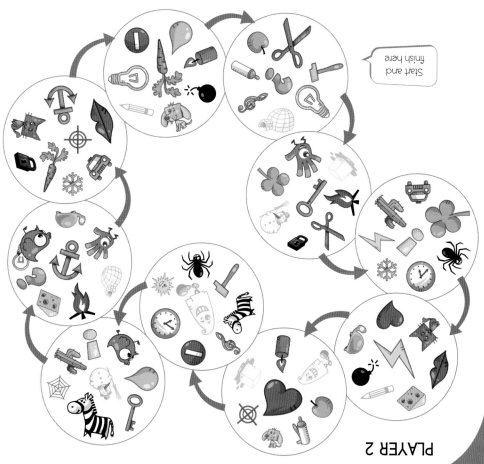

Start and finish here

PLAYER 2

51

# Spot It!

Add a horizontal, vertical or diagonal arrow to each empty square. The symbols indicate how many arrows should be pointing to them and each arrow can point to more than one symbol.

 1 arrow   2 arrows   3 arrows

 4 arrows   5 arrows   6 arrows

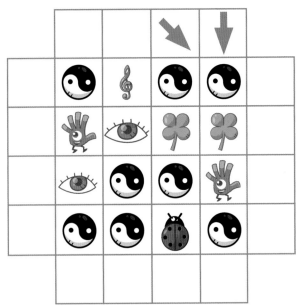

Shady Business

Which of these silhouettes is an accurate representation of this image?

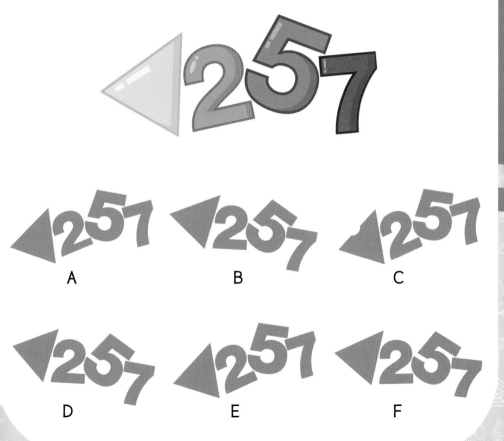

A

B

C

D

E

F

Find the Pair

Which Spot It! symbol appears twice in this jumble?

A Trespasser

Find the intruder among these Spot It! symbols.

 # Chartreuse Calculation

🍀 + 🌵 + 🌵 = 48

0 = 🌳 x 🍎

🌵 ÷ 🌳 = 🌳

🌵 = 🍀

🌳 + 🍎 + 🍀 + 🌵 = ❓

What is the value of each symbol?

Off the Grid

Unscramble these Spot It! symbols and enter the correct grid references in the blank grid as shown below.

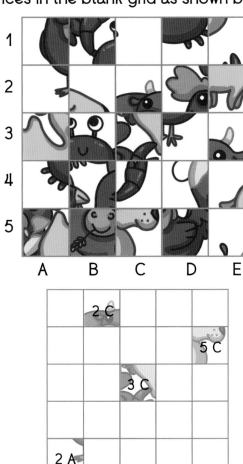

1 2 3 4 5

A B C D E

	2 C			
				5 C
		3 C		
2 A				

Odd One Out

Which Spot It! symbol is the odd one out?

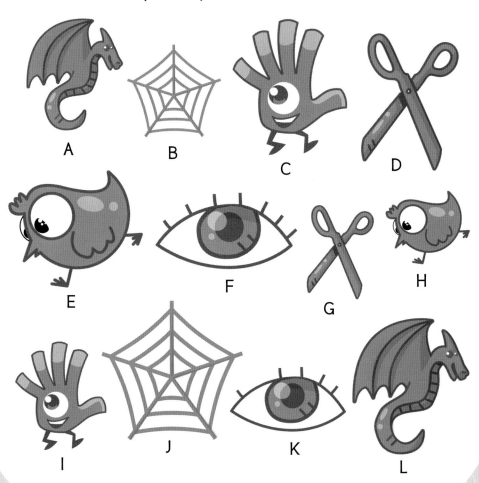

A

B

C

D

E

F

G

H

I

J

K

L

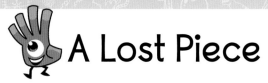

A Lost Piece

Which of the fragments below fit into
the missing spaces?

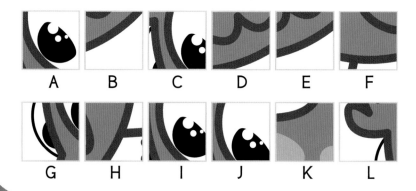

A B C D E F

G H I J K L

Seeing Double

Which Spot It! symbol appears only once in this jumble?

Make a Loop:
a game for 2 players

PLAYER 1

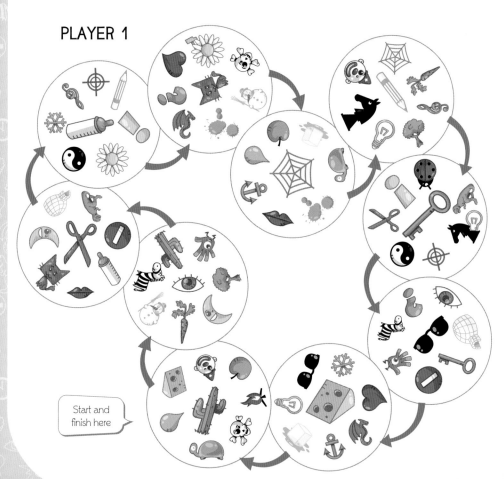

Start and finish here

How to play:

Lay the book between the two players so that both can see their own page. In classic Spot It! style, you progress by finding the identical symbol between a card and the next one along the trail. The winner of this head-to-head contest is the first player to make a complete loop back to their starting card.

Ready? On your marks, get set... GO!

Start and finish here

PLAYER 2

61

Follow That Hand!

Create a loop that passes through every symbol.
The loop doesn't have to turn in a square, but if it does then it can only move in the direction indicated by the symbol: the Spot It! symbol means up, the Dinosaur means left, the Dragon means right, and the Spider means down.
It must not enter the empty yellow square.

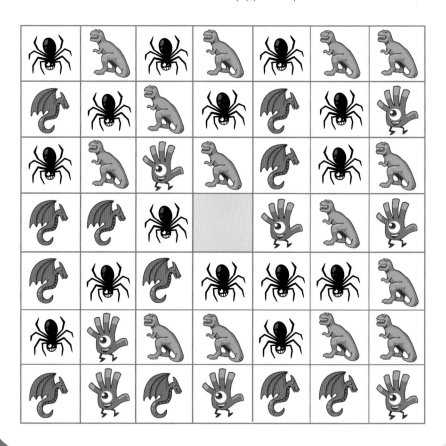

Shady Business

Which of these silhouettes is an accurate reflection of this scene?

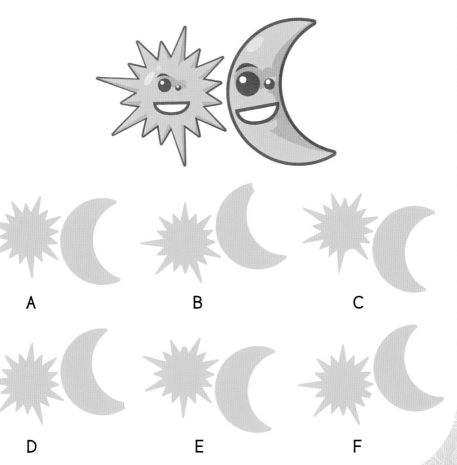

A

B

C

D

E

F

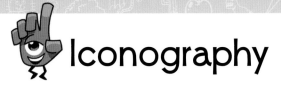 Iconography

Divide these symbols into sections by drawing lines so that each section contains one of each symbol.

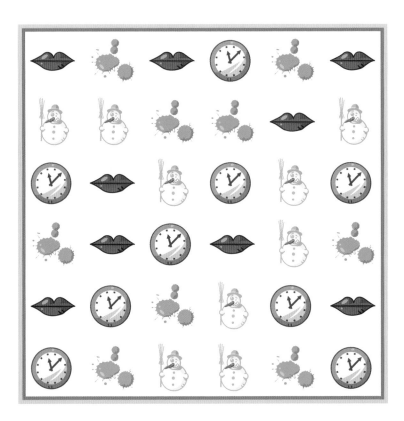

Mirrors

Which two collections of Spot It! symbols are
exact mirror images?

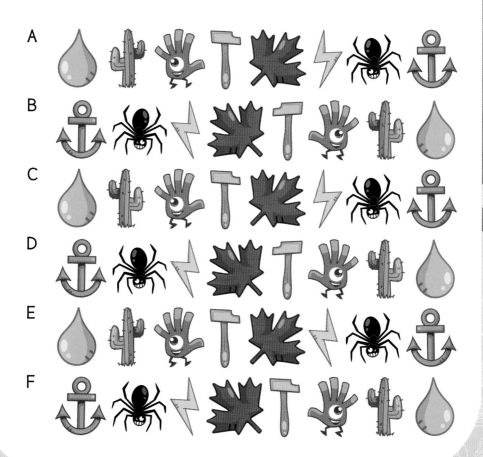

A

B

C

D

E

F

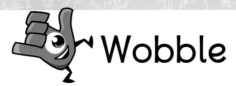

Wobble

Which square is wrong, and why?

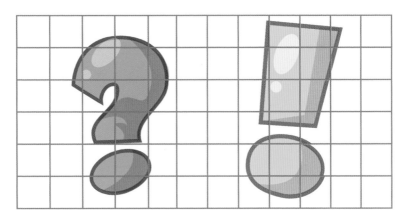

Spot (It!) the Difference

Spot the six differences between these two Spot It! cards.

Find the Pair

Which Spot It! symbol appears twice in this jumble?

Make a Loop:
a game for 2 players

PLAYER 1

Start and finish here

How to play:

Lay the book between the two players so that both can see their own page. In classic Spot It! style, you progress by finding the identical symbol between a card and the next one along the trail. The winner of this head-to-head contest is the first player to make a complete loop back to their starting card.

Ready? On your marks, get set... GO!

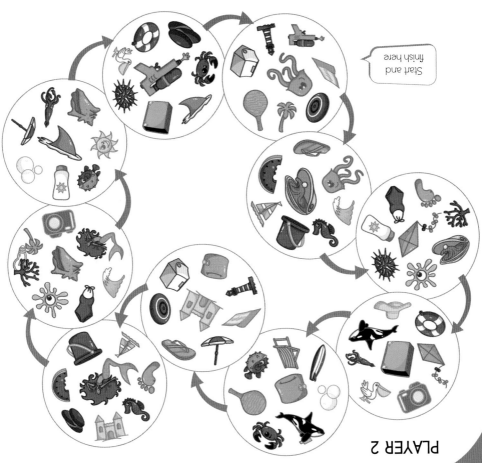

Start and finish here

PLAYER 2

69

Dividing Lines

Add four straight lines to divide the box below so that each Dinosaur has its own section.

Off the Grid

Put these Spot It! symbols back together by entering the correct grid references in the blank grid, as shown below.

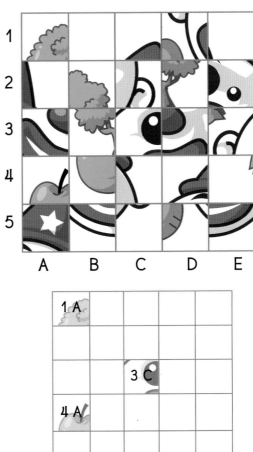

 # Spot It!

Add a horizontal, vertical or diagonal arrow to each empty square. The symbols indicate how many arrows should be pointing to them and each arrow can point to more than one symbol.

 1 arrow

 2 arrows

 3 arrows

 4 arrows

 5 arrows

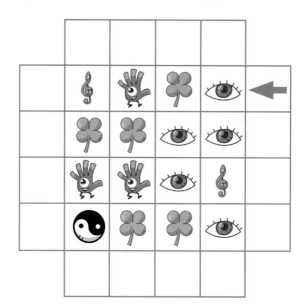

Odd One Out

Which Spot It! symbol is the odd one out?

A

B

C

D

E

F

G

H

I

J

K

L

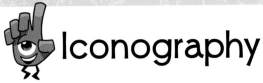# Iconography

Divide these symbols into sections by drawing lines so that each section contains one of each symbol.

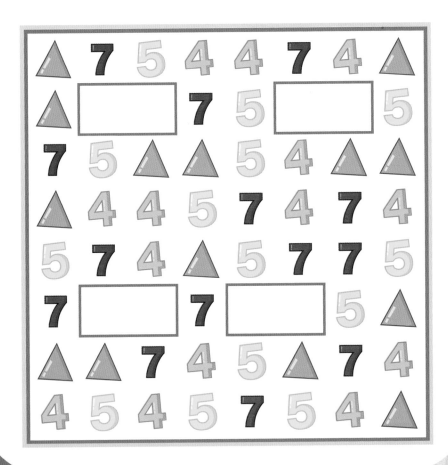

A Trespasser

Find the intruder among these Spot It! symbols.

Spot (It!) the Difference

Spot the six differences between these two Spot It! cards.

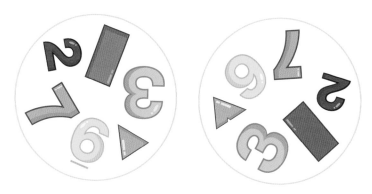

Seeing Double

Which Spot It! symbol appears only once in this jumble?

Fierce Competition

These Spot It! symbols are playing tug of war, but they're evenly matched. In the first contest, four Snowmen have tied against five Dinosaurs.

In the next contest, one Man has tied against two Dinosaurs and one Snowman.

In the final contest, one Man and three Dinosaurs will be playing against four Snowmen. Work out the relative strength of each symbol to find who will win.

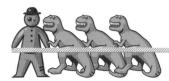 

Shady Business

Which of these silhouettes is an accurate reflection of the Mermaid symbol?

A

B

C

D

E

F

Find the Pair

Which Spot It! symbol appears twice in this jumble?

Make a Loop:
a game for 2 players

PLAYER 1

Start and finish here

How to play:

Lay the book between the two players so that both can see their own page. In classic Spot It! style, you progress by finding the identical symbol between a card and the next one along the trail. The winner of this head-to-head contest is the first player to make a complete loop back to their starting card.

Ready? On your marks, get set... GO!

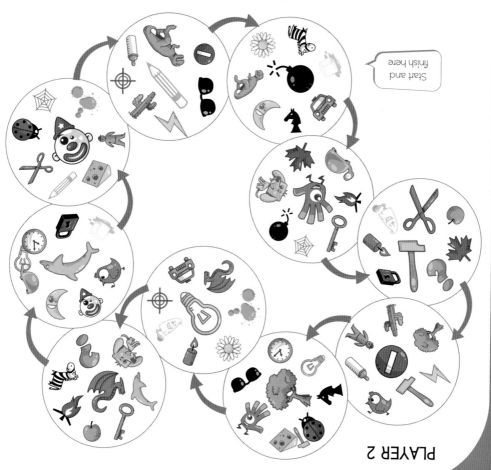

Start and finish here

PLAYER 2

81

Spot It!

Add a horizontal, vertical or diagonal arrow to each empty square. The symbols indicate how many arrows should be pointing to them and each arrow can point to more than one symbol.

 1 arrow

 2 arrows

 3 arrows

 4 arrows

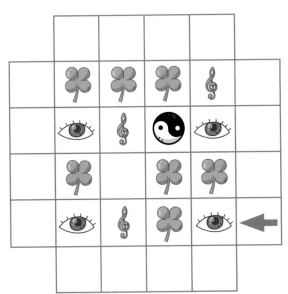

Odd One Out

Which Spot It! symbol is the odd one out?

Mirrors

Which two collections of Spot It! symbols are exact mirror images?

A

B

C

D

E

F

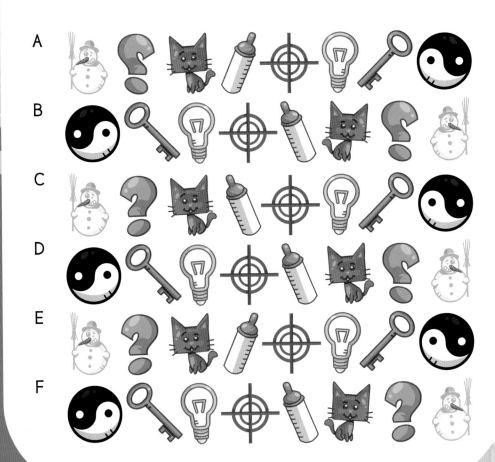

Off the Grid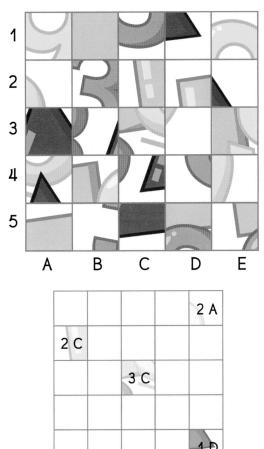

Unscramble these Spot It! symbols and enter the correct grid references in the blank grid as shown below.

Wobble

Which square doesn't follow the same logic as the other squares, and why?

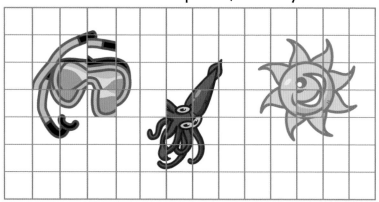

 A Trespasser

Find the intruder among these Spot It! symbols.

Iconography

Divide these symbols into sections by drawing lines so that each section contains one of each symbol.

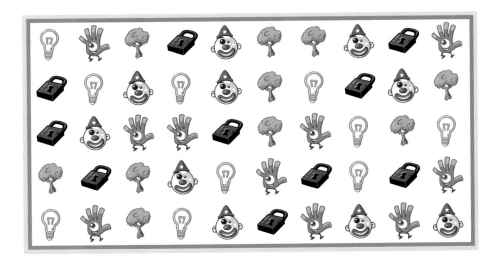

Shady Business

Which of these silhouettes is an accurate reflection of this scene?

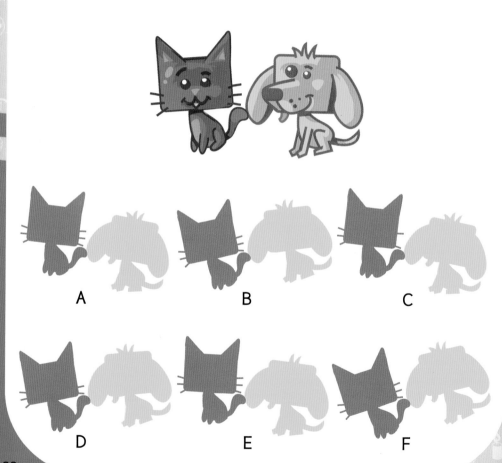

A

B

C

D

E

F

Spot It!

Add a horizontal, vertical or diagonal arrow to each empty square. The symbols indicate how many arrows should be pointing to them and each arrow can point to more than one symbol.

 1 arrow   2 arrows

 3 arrows   5 arrows

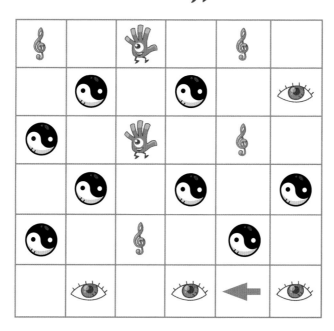

Make a Loop:
a game for 2 players

PLAYER 1

Start and finish here

How to play:

Lay the book between the two players so that both can see their own page. In classic Spot It! style, you progress by finding the identical symbol between a card and the next one along the trail. The winner of this head-to-head contest is the first player to make a complete loop back to their starting card.

Ready? On your marks, get set... GO!

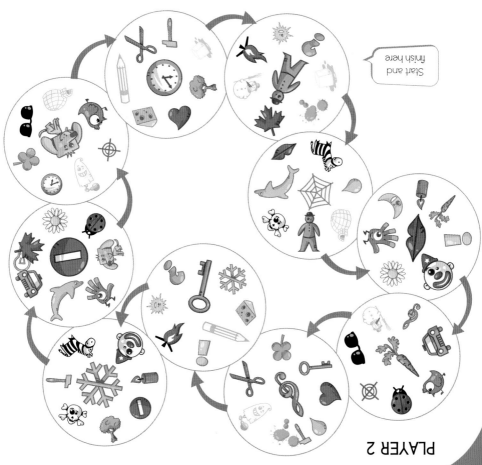

Start and finish here

PLAYER 2

91

Seeing Double

Which Spot It! symbol appears only once in this jumble?

A Lost Piece

Which of the fragments below fit into the missing spaces?

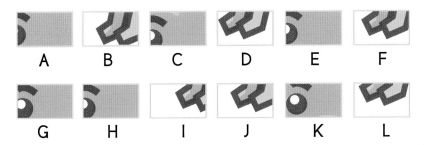

A   B   C   D   E   F

G   H   I   J   K   L

Mirrors

Which two collections of Spot It! symbols are exact mirror images?

A

B

C

D

E

F

Find the Pair

Which Spot It! symbol appears twice in this jumble?

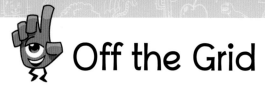

Off the Grid

Unscramble these Spot It! symbols and enter the correct grid references in the blank grid as shown below.

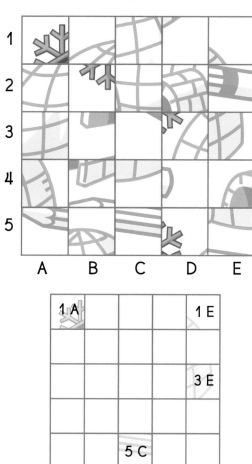

Spot (It!) the Difference

Spot the six differences between these two Spot It! cards.

Aquatic Addition

What is each of the three symbols worth?

$$\text{❄} + \text{🧊} = \text{💧} + 3$$

$$\text{💧} = \text{❄} + 7$$

$$1 = \text{🧊} \div \text{❄}$$

Odd One Out

Which Spot It! symbol is the odd one out?

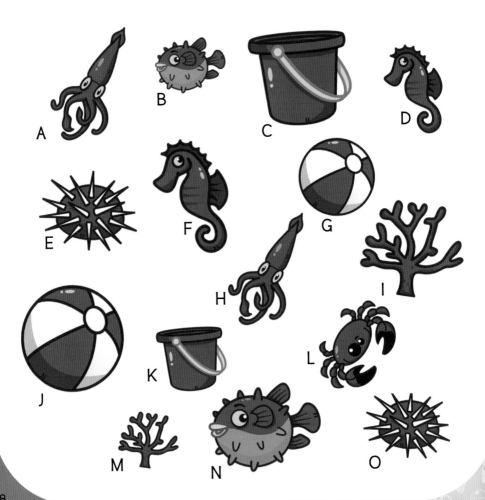

A

B

C

D

E

F

G

H

I

J

K

L

M

N

O

Follow That Hand!

Create a loop that passes through every symbol. The loop doesn't have to turn in a square, but if it does then it can only move in the direction indicated by the symbol: the Spot It! symbol means up, the Dinosaur means left, the Dragon means right, and the Spider means down.

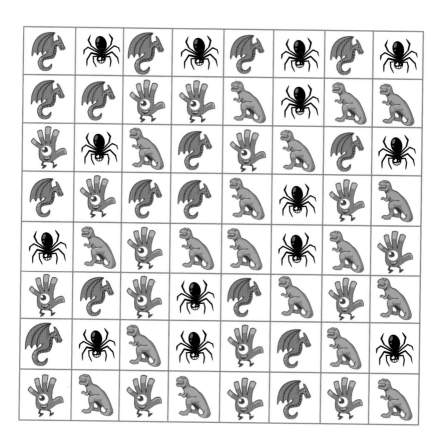

Make a Loop:
a game for 2 players

PLAYER 1

Start and
finish here

100

How to play:

Lay the book between the two players so that both can see their own page. In classic Spot It! style, you progress by finding the identical symbol between a card and the next one along the trail. The winner of this head-to-head contest is the first player to make a complete loop back to their starting card.

Ready? On your marks, get set... GO!

Start and finish here

PLAYER 2

101

Dividing Lines

Add five straight lines to divide the box below so that each symbol has its own section.

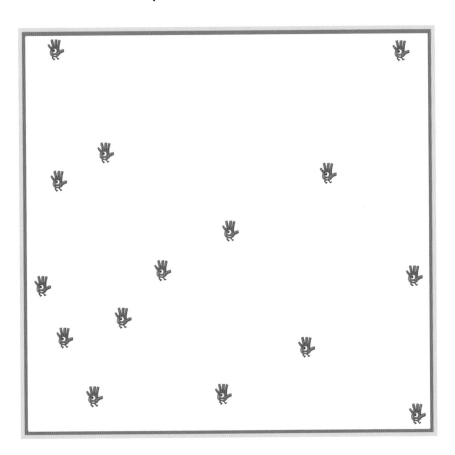

Shady Business

Which of these silhouettes is an accurate reflection of these animal symbols?

A

B

C

D

E

F

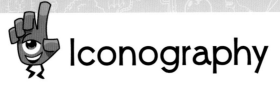

Iconography

Divide these symbols into sections so that every region contains exactly one of each symbol.

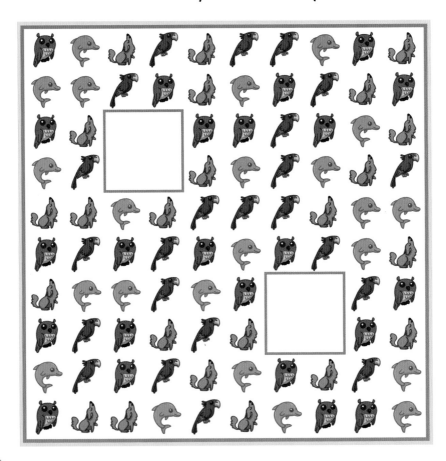

Spot It!

Add a horizontal, vertical or diagonal arrow to each empty square. The symbols indicate how many arrows should be pointing to them and each arrow can point to more than one symbol.

 1 arrow   2 arrows

 3 arrows   4 arrows

 5 arrows   6 arrows

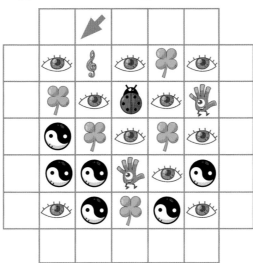

Mirrors

Which two collections of Spot It! symbols are exact mirror images?

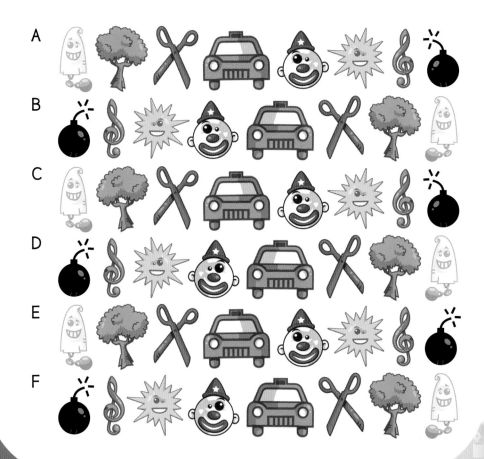

A

B

C

D

E

F

Seeing Double

Which Spot It! symbol appears only once in this jumble?

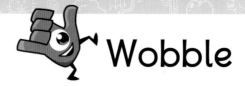

Wobble

Which square doesn't follow the same logic as the other squares, and why?

Spot (It!) the Difference

Spot the six differences between these two Spot It! cards.

Winning Ways

You can take home as many of these Spot It! symbols as you'd like, but their total must be exactly 50. Which ones will you choose?

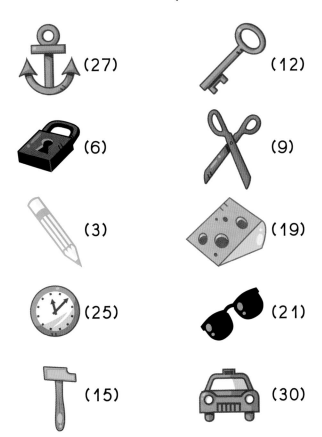

(27) (12)

(6) (9)

(3) (19)

(25) (21)

(15) (30)

Make a Loop:
a game for 2 players

PLAYER 1

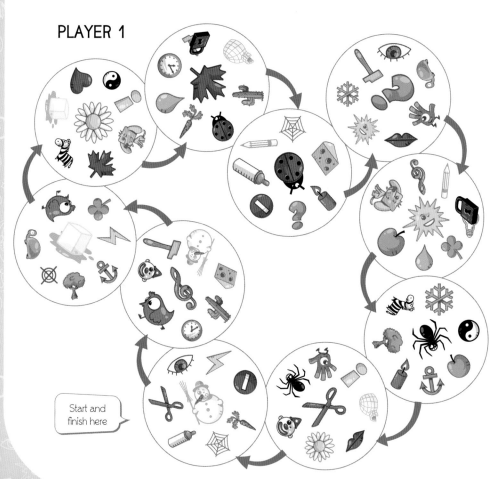

Start and finish here

110

How to play:

Lay the book between the two players so that both can see their own page. In classic Spot It! style, you progress by finding the identical symbol between a card and the next one along the trail. The winner of this head-to-head contest is the first player to make a complete loop back to their starting card.

Ready? On your marks, get set... GO!

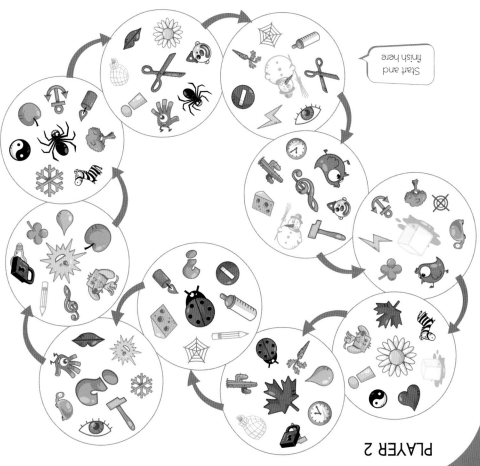

Start and finish here

PLAYER 2

111

Find the Pair

Which Spot It! symbol appears twice in this jumble?

Off the Grid

Unscramble these Spot It! symbols and enter the correct grid references in the blank grid as shown below.

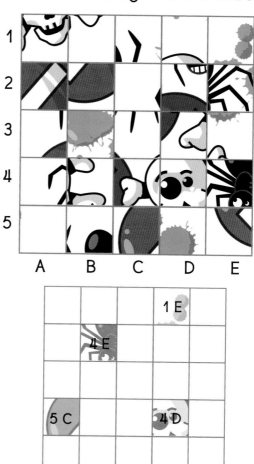

1 E

4 E

5 C

4 D

Shady Business

Which of these silhouettes is an accurate reflection of this aquatic scene?

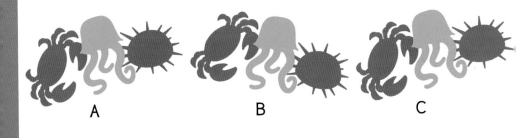

A   B   C

D   E   F

Odd One Out

Which Spot It! symbol is the odd one out?

A   B   C

D   E   F

G   H

# Spot It!

Add a horizontal, vertical or diagonal arrow to each empty square. The symbols indicate how many arrows should be pointing to them and each arrow can point to more than one symbol.

 0 arrows   1 arrow   2 arrows

3 arrows   4 arrows   5 arrows

6 arrows   7 arrows

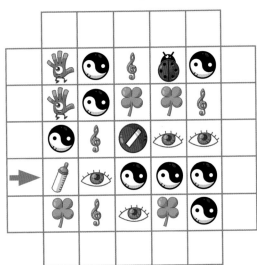

Monochrome Multiplication

What is the value of each icon?

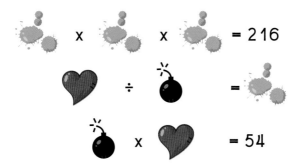

$$\text{splat} \times \text{splat} \times \text{splat} = 216$$

$$\text{heart} \div \text{bomb} = \text{splat}$$

$$\text{bomb} \times \text{heart} = 54$$

A Trespasser

Find the intruder among these Spot It! symbols.

Make a Loop:
a game for 2 players

PLAYER 1

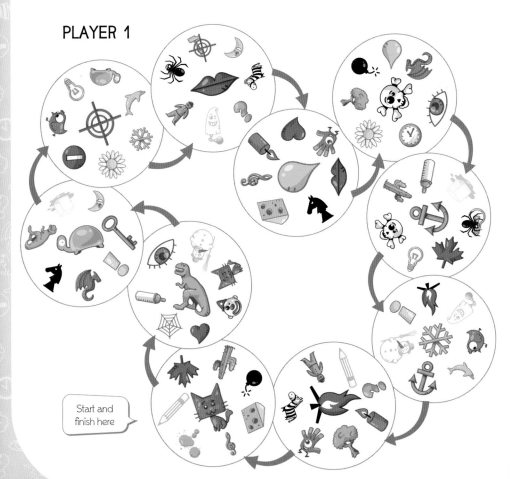

Start and finish here

How to play:

Lay the book between the two players so that both can see their own page. In classic Spot It! style, you progress by finding the identical symbol between a card and the next one along the trail. The winner of this head-to-head contest is the first player to make a complete loop back to their starting card.

Ready? On your marks, get set... GO!

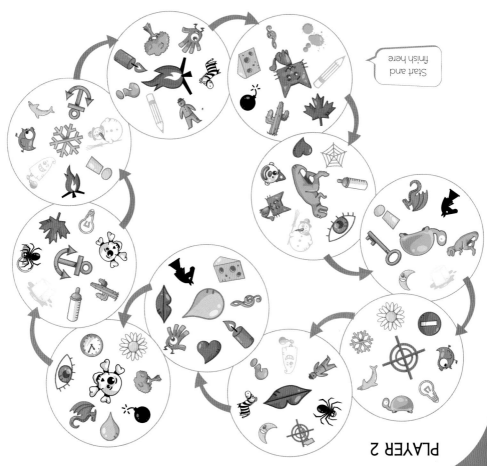

Start and finish here

PLAYER 2

119

Mirrors

Which two collections of Spot It! symbols are exact mirror images?

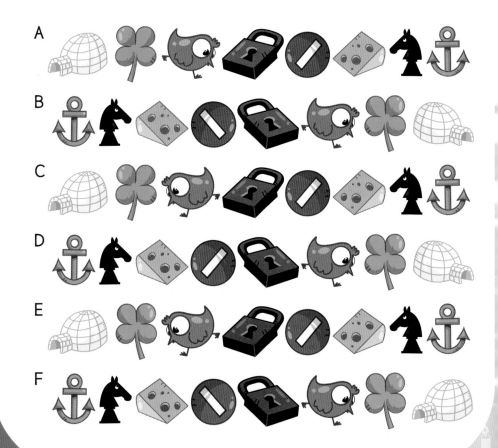

A

B

C

D

E

F

A Lost Piece

Which of the fragments below fit into the missing spaces?

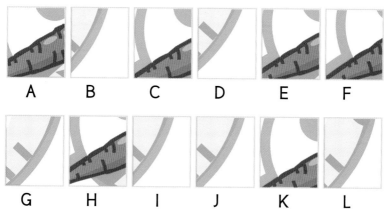

A   B   C   D   E   F

G   H   I   J   K   L

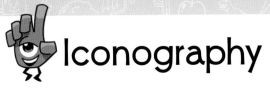

Iconography

Divide these symbols into sections by drawing lines so that each section contains one of each symbol.

Seeing Spot It!

Which Spot It! symbol appears only once in this jumble?

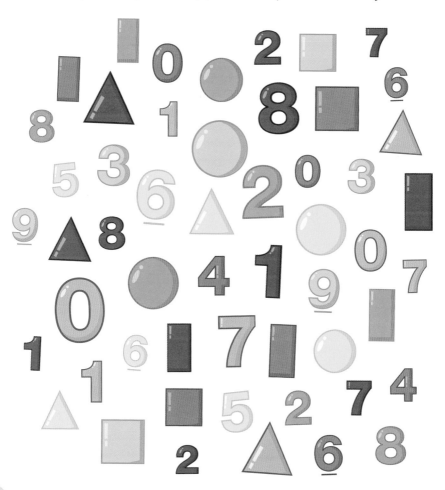

Dividing Lines

Add six straight lines to divide the box below so that each Apple has its own section.

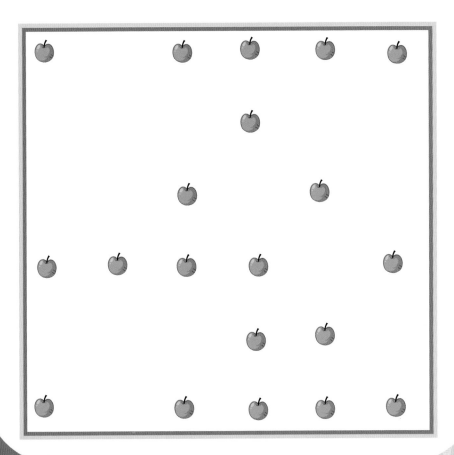

Follow That Hand!

Create a loop that passes through every symbol. The loop doesn't have to turn in a square, but if it does then it can only move in the direction indicated by the symbol: the Spot It! symbol means up, the Dinosaur means left, the Dragon means right, the Spider means down, and the Target means any direction.

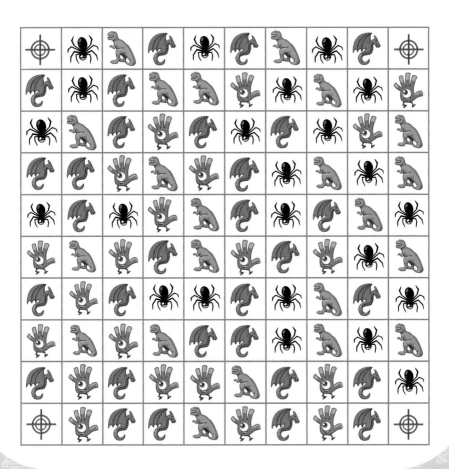

Double Trouble

Which Spot It! symbol appears twice in this jumble?

Off the Grid

Put this Spot It! symbol back together by entering the correct grid references in the blank grid as shown below.

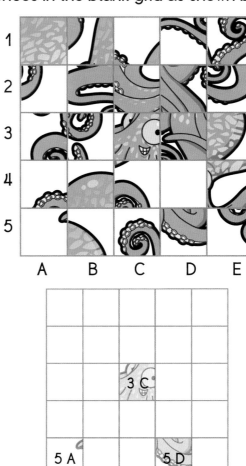

Make a Loop:
a game for 2 players

PLAYER 1

Start and finish here

How to play:

Lay the book between the two players so that both can see their own page. In classic Spot It! style, you progress by finding the identical symbol between a card and the next one along the trail. The winner of this head-to-head contest is the first player to make a complete loop back to their starting card.

Ready? On your marks, get set... GO!

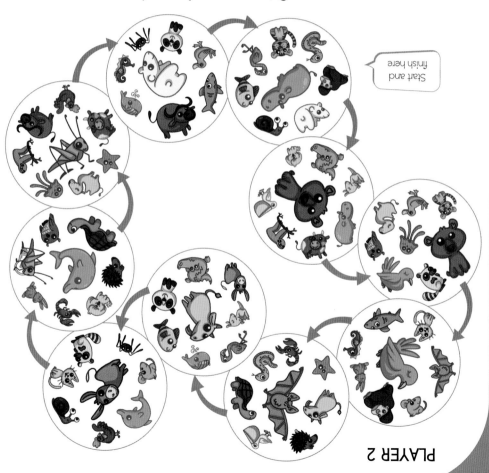

Start and finish here

PLAYER 2

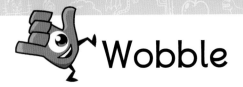

Wobble

Which square is wrong, and why?

Spot (It!) the Difference

Spot the six differences between these two Spot It! cards.

Spot It!

Add a horizontal, vertical or diagonal arrow to each empty square. The symbols indicate how many arrows should be pointing to them and each arrow can point to more than one symbol.

 1 arrow   2 arrows   3 arrows

 4 arrows   5 arrows

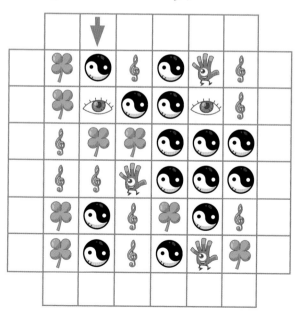

Odd One Out

Which Spot It! symbol is the odd one out?

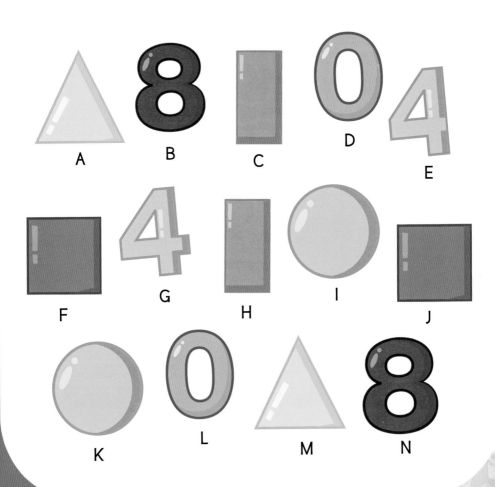

A

B

C

D

E

F

G

H

I

J

K

L

M

N

Stop?!

Place the numbers 1–2 under each symbol so that the central columns, central rows, all of the Exclamation marks together, all of the Question marks together and all of the Stop signs together each add up to the same number.

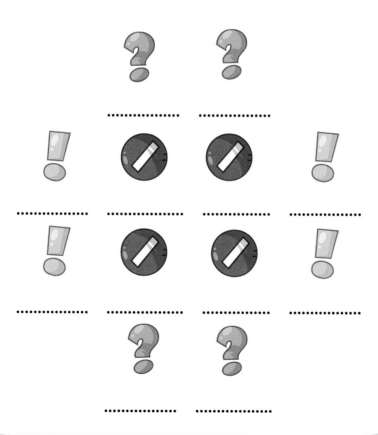

Iconography

Divide these symbols into sections by drawing lines so that each section contains one of each symbol.

Shady Business

Which of these silhouettes is an accurate reflection of this scene?

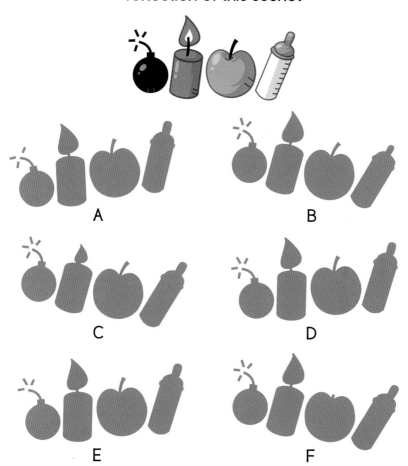

A

B

C

D

E

F

Seeing Double

Which Spot It! symbol appears only once in this jumble?

A Trespasser

Find the intruder among these Spot It! symbols.

Purple Problem

What is each of the three symbols worth?

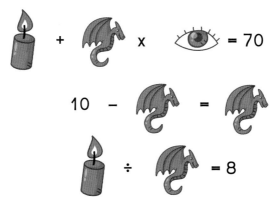

Make a Loop:
a game for 2 players

PLAYER 1

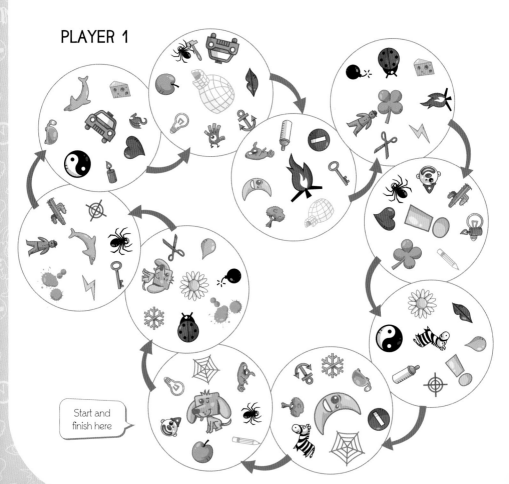

Start and finish here

How to play:

Lay the book between the two players so that both can see their own page. In classic Spot It! style, you progress by finding the identical symbol between a card and the next one along the trail. The winner of this head-to-head contest is the first player to make a complete loop back to their starting card.

Ready? On your marks, get set... GO!

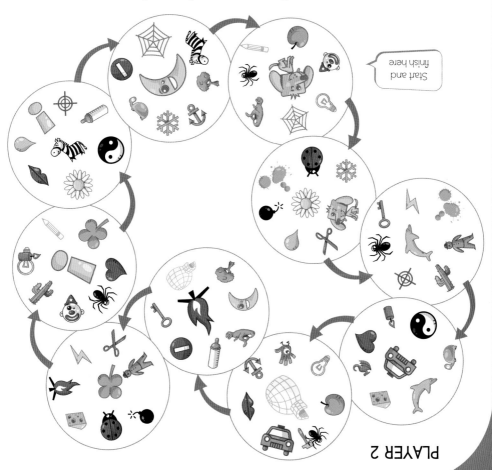

Start and finish here

PLAYER 2

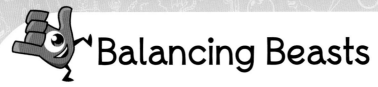

Balancing Beasts

One frog and six rabbits weigh the same as one hedgehog.

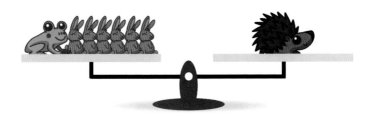

But also: three frogs and a hedgehog weigh the same as ten rabbits.

How many rabbits would weigh as much as one hedgehog?

Mirrors

Which two collections of Spot It! symbols are exact mirror images?

A

B

C

D

E

F

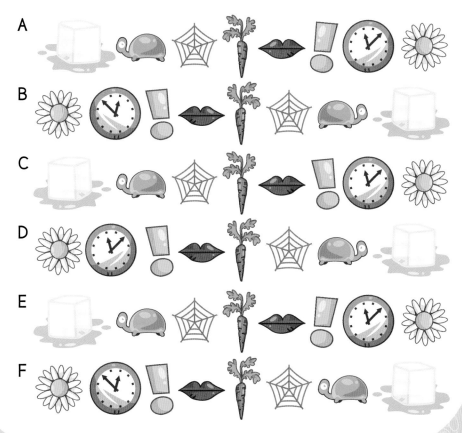

Spot It!

Add a horizontal, vertical or diagonal arrow to each empty square. The symbols indicate how many arrows should be pointing to them and each arrow can point to more than one symbol.

 1 arrow   2 arrows   3 arrows

 4 arrows   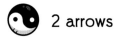 5 arrows   6 arrows

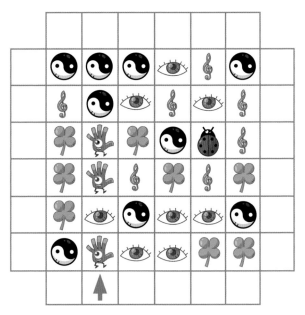

The Missing Link

Which symbol should appear in the empty space?

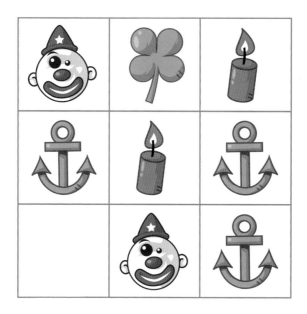

1   2   3   4   5

Dividing Lines

Divide this grid into four identical, equally-sized shapes that each contain one Dog and one Cat.

Off the Grid

Unscramble these Spot It! symbols and enter the
correct grid references in the blank grid, as shown below.

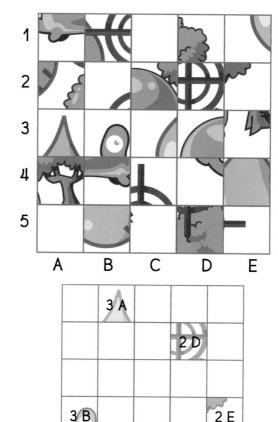

Spot (It!) the Difference

Spot the six differences between these two Spot It! cards.

 Wobble

Which squares are wrong, and why?

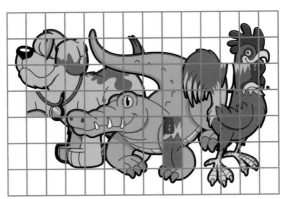

Find the Pair

Which Spot It! symbol appears twice in this jumble?

Make a Loop:
a game for 2 players

PLAYER 1

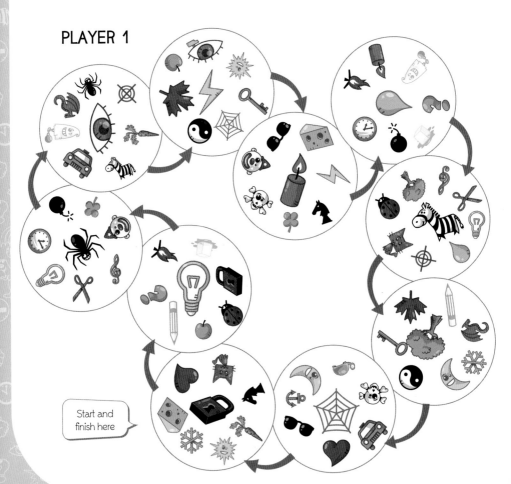

Start and finish here

148

How to play:

Lay the book between the two players so that both can see their own page. In classic Spot It! style, you progress by finding the identical symbol between a card and the next one along the trail. The winner of this head-to-head contest is the first player to make a complete loop back to their starting card.

Ready? On your marks, get set... GO!

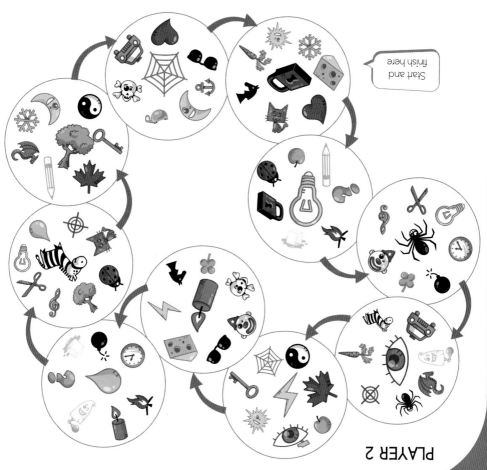

Start and
finish here

PLAYER 2

149

Solutions

PAGE 5: Seeing Double
The Treble Clef.

PAGE 6: Iconography

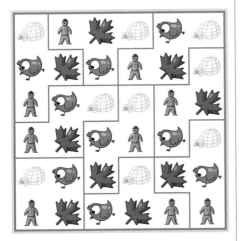

PAGE 7: A Lost Piece
E and J.

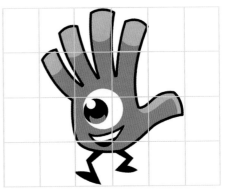

PAGE 10: Wobble

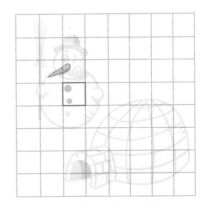

The highlighted square has
been flipped vertically.

PAGE 10: Spot (It!) the Difference

PAGE 11: Shady Business
D.

PAGE 12: Find the Pair
The Hammer.

PAGE 13: Odd One Out

PAGE 14: Mirrors
C and F.

A
B
C
D
E
F

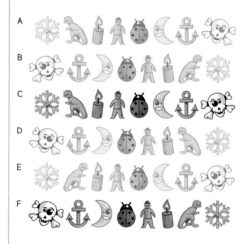

PAGE 15: Off the Grid

1 A	3 C	5 E	3 B	1 C
3 A	3 E	3 D	5 D	2 E
1 E	4 E	1 D	4 A	4 C
2 A	1 B	2 C	4 D	2 D
5 C	5 B	2 B	5 A	4 B

PAGE 16: Spot It!

PAGE 17: Seeing Double
The Apple.

PAGE 20: Spot (It!)
the Difference

PAGE 20: A Trespasser
The Spider (it is from the Spot It! Animals set, not the original game).

PAGE 21: Iconography

PAGE 23: Odd One Out

PAGE 22: Shady Business
F.

PAGE 24: Find the Pair
The Duck.

PAGE 25: Follow That Hand!

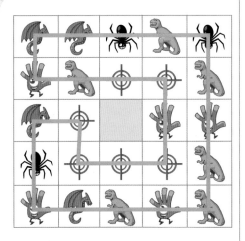

PAGE 27: Wobble

This square has been rotated counterclockwise instead of clockwise, as the other three have been.

PAGE 26: Mirrors
D and E.

PAGE 27: A Trespasser
The Rectangle (all the rest are numbers).

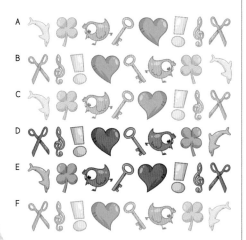

154

PAGE 30: Off the Grid

3 A	1 C	5 E	1 D	1 E
2 A	1 A	3 C	5 C	4 D
4 C	3 B	2 C	1 B	3 E
2 D	4 B	4 E	4 A	3 D
5 D	5 A	2 B	5 B	2 E

PAGE 31: Spot It!

PAGE 32: A Lost Piece
E and J.

PAGE 33: Seeing Double
The Seal.

PAGE 34: Odd One Out

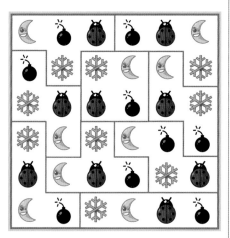

PAGE 35: Iconography

PAGE 36: Shady Business
B.

PAGE 37: Mirrors
A and D

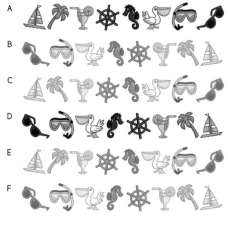

PAGE 38: Spot (It!)
the Difference

PAGE 42: Dividing Lines

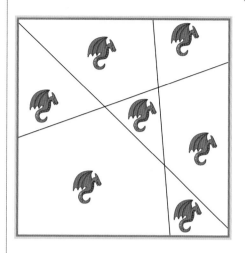

PAGE 38: Summer Sums

Sun = 8

Daisy = 25

 Sunglasses = 25

PAGE 39: Find the Pair
The Clown.

PAGE 43: Off the Grid

3 C	5 A	1 A	1 E	1 C
4 D	2 E	2 D	3 B	4 E
1 D	5 C	2 A	5 D	4 A
3 A	5 B	4 C	1 B	3 D
2 C	3 E	2 B	5 E	4 B

PAGE 44: Odd One Out

PAGE 45: Seeing Double
The Ladybird.

PAGE 46: Follow That Hand!

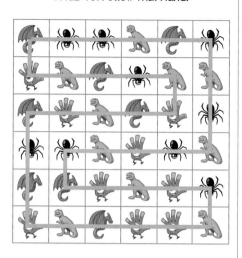

PAGE 47: Iconography

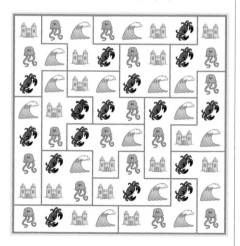

Page 48: Wobble

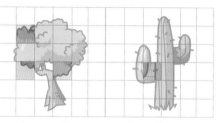

The purple square has been flipped horizontally instead of vertically, as the three orange squares have been.

PAGE 48: Spot (It!)
the Difference

PAGE 49: Mirrors
E and F.

A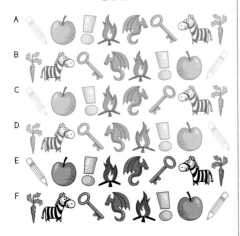

B

C

D

E

F

Page 52: Spot It!

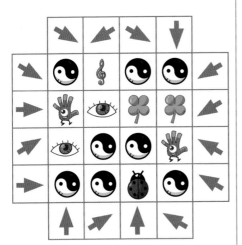

Page 53: Shady Business
E.

Page 54: Find the Pair
The Orange circle.

Page 55: A Trespasser
The Turtle (it is from the original Spot It! set, not the Spot It! Kids set, as the other symbols are).

Page 55: Chartreuse Calculation

 Cactus = 16

 Clover = 16

 Apple = 0

Tree = 4

 Question mark = 36

PAGE 56: Off the Grid

5 E	2 C	3 E	4 E	2 B
4 D	5 B	5 A	3 A	5 C
2 D	4 B	3 C	2 E	1 E
1 A	5 D	1 B	3 B	4 C
2 A	3 D	4 A	1 D	1 C

Page 57: Odd One Out

Page 58: A Lost Piece
E and J.

Page 59: Seeing Double
The Elephant.

PAGE 62: Follow That Hand!

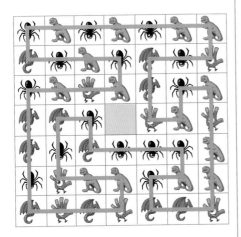

PAGE 64: Iconography

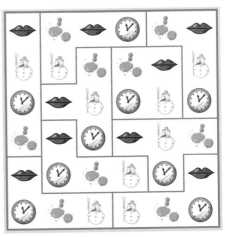

PAGE 63: Shady Business
A.

PAGE 65: Mirrors
A and B.

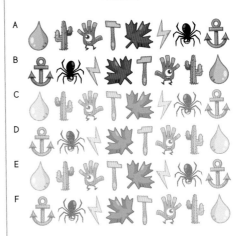

PAGE 66: Wobble

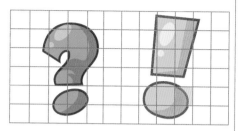

The orange square has had its dimensions changed.

PAGE 66: Spot (It!)
the Difference

PAGE 67: Find the Pair
The Pencil.

PAGE 70: Dividing Lines

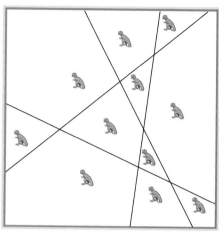

PAGE 7 1: Off the Grid

1 A	2 B	1 B	1 C	1 E
3 B	2 D	4 D	5 A	2 A
4 E	3 E	3 C	2 E	4 C
4 A	1 D	3 A	3 D	2 C
4 B	5 D	5 B	5 E	5 C

PAGE 72: Spot It!

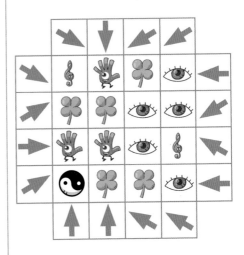

PAGE 73: Odd One Out

164

PAGE 74: Iconography

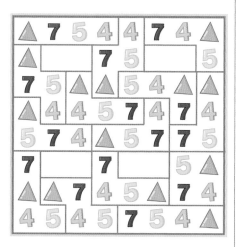

PAGE 75: A Trespasser

The Lock (it is from the original Spot It! set, not the Spot It! Waterproof set, as the other symbols are).

PAGE 75: Spot (It!) the Difference

PAGE 76: Seeing Double

The Exclamation Mark.

PAGE 77: Fierce Competition

The Man and the three Dinosaurs will win. In the final contest the Man can be replaced by two Dinosaurs and a Snowman, as the second contest demonstrates that they're evenly matched (meaning a Man is stronger than a Dinosaur or a Snowman). This would make the final contest five Dinosaurs and a Snowman against four Snowmen. We know from the first contest that five Dinosaurs and four Snowmen are evenly matched (meaning a Snowman is stronger than a Dinosaur), so they cancel each other out, leaving the extra strength of the Snowman on the left to win.

PAGE 78: Shady Business
C.

PAGE 79: Find the Pair
The Eagle.

PAGE 82: Spot It!

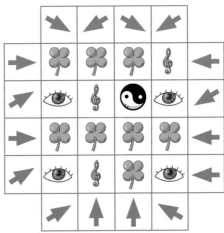

PAGE 83: Odd One Out

PAGE 84: Mirrors
B and E.

A
B
C
D
E
F

PAGE 85: Off the Grid

2 D	5 A	4 B	1 E	2 A
2 C	1 B	3 E	1 A	4 E
5 E	5 D	3 C	4 A	3 D
5 B	2 B	3 B	3 A	2 E
4 D	1 C	4 C	5 C	1 D

PAGE 86: Wobble

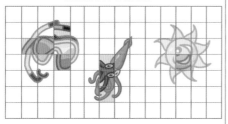

All of the orange squares have been alternately rotated clockwise and counterclockwise along rows, except for the one highlighted in purple.

PAGE 86: A Trespasser

The Dragon (it is from the original Spot It! set, not the Spot It! Kids set, as the other symbols are).

PAGE 87: Iconography

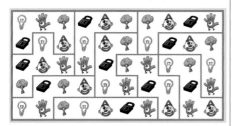

PAGE 88: Shady Business
F.

PAGE 89: Spot It!

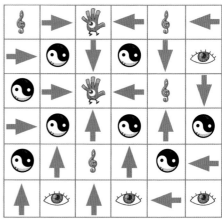

PAGE 92: Seeing Double
The Coral.

PAGE 93: A Lost Piece
B and E.

PAGE 94: Mirrors
A and F.

PAGE 95: Double Trouble
The Lightbulb.

PAGE 96: Off the Grid

1 A	5 D	1 B	5 B	1 E
2 B	3 D	2 A	1 C	4 A
4 E	2 D	2 C	3 A	3 E
3 B	4 B	5 E	4 C	1 D
3 C	5 A	5 C	2 E	4 D

PAGE 97: Spot (It!)
the Difference

PAGE 98: Odd One Out

PAGE 97: Aquatic Addition

 Snowflake = 10

 Teardrop = 17

 Ice cube = 10

PAGE 99: Follow That Hand!

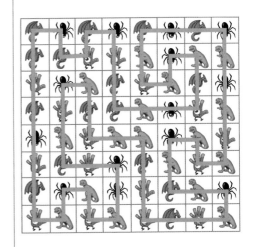

PAGE 102: Dividing Lines

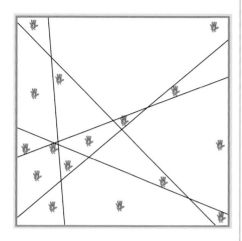

PAGE 104: Iconography

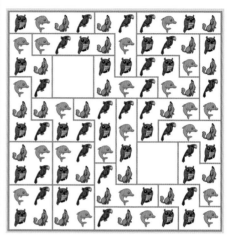

PAGE 103: Shady Business

E.

PAGE 105: Spot It!

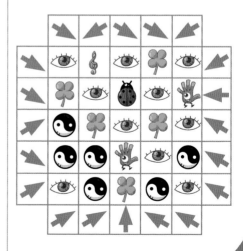

PAGE 106: Mirrors
C and D.

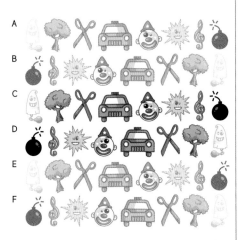

Page 107: Seeing Double
The Turtle.

PAGE 108: Wobble

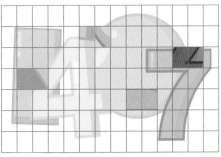

All of the orange squares have been alternately rotated clockwise and counterclockwise along rows, except for the one highlighted in purple.

PAGE 108: Spot (It!)
the Difference

PAGE 109: Winning Ways

 The Clock (25),

 Cheese (19),

 and Lock (6).

PAGE 114: Find the Pair
The Palm Tree

PAGE 113: Off the Grid

2 C	5 B	1 C	1 E	5 A
4 A	4 E	2 E	3 B	5 D
3 A	2 D	3 C	1 D	3 E
5 C	2 A	4 C	4 D	4 B
5 E	2 B	3 D	1 A	1 B

PAGE 114: Shady Business
A.

PAGE 115: Odd One Out

PAGE 116: Spot It!

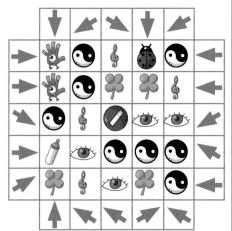

PAGE 117: Monochrome Multiplication

 Splotch = 6

 Heart = 18

Bomb = 3

PAGE 117: A Trespasser

The Camel (it is from the Spot It! Kids set, not the Animals set, as the other symbols are).

PAGE 120: Mirrors

B and C.

PAGE 121: A Lost Piece
F and G.

PAGE 123: Seeing Double
The Circle.

PAGE 124: Dividing Lines

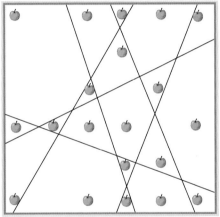

PAGE 122: Iconography

PAGE 125: Follow That Hand!

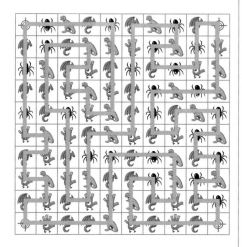

PAGE 127: Off the Grid

4 D	4 A	1 C	4 B	5 B
5 C	1 E	1 B	1 A	3 E
3 A	2 C	3 C	4 E	4 C
5 E	2 B	3 D	2 D	3 B
5 A	1 D	2 E	5 D	2 A

PAGE 126: Find the Pair
The Clock.

PAGE 130: Wobble

All the orange squares have been flipped horizontally around, but the purple square has remained in place.

PAGE 130: Spot (It!)
the Difference

PAGE 131: Spot It!

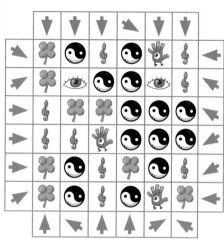

PAGE 132: Odd One Out

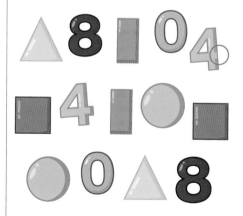

PAGE 133: Stop?!

Each grouping should add up to 26. Here's one possible arrangement:

PAGE 134: Iconography

PAGE 135: Shady Business

D.

PAGE 136: Seeing Double

The Flower.

PAGE 137: A Trespasser

Dobbly (the other symbols are from the original Spot It! set, but this symbol is not).

PAGE 137: Purple Problem

 Dragon = 5

 Candle = 40

 Eye = 6

PAGE 140: Balancing Beasts

It would take seven rabbits to match the weight of one hedgehog. 1 hedgehog equals 1 frog and 6 rabbits, and 3 frogs and 1 hedgehog equals 10 rabbits, so if you replaced the hedgehog with 1 frog and 6 rabbits, then 4 frogs and 6 rabbits would equal 10 rabbits. Frogs and rabbits therefore weigh the same, so if you replace the original frog you'd have 7 rabbits equaling one hedgehog.

PAGE 141: Mirrors

B and E.

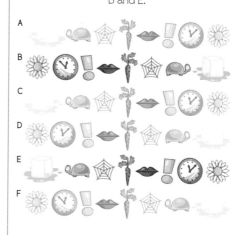

PAGE 142: Spot It!

PAGE 143: The Missing Link

The Clown. If you replace the grid symbols with their accompanying numbers then each row and column will add up to 10.

PAGE 144: Mirrors

PAGE 145: Off the Grid

5 A	3 A	2 B	4 C	1 C
3 C	4 E	1 B	2 D	5 E
1 E	5 B	2 A	5 D	1 D
3 B	3 D	2 C	4 A	2 E
4 D	1 A	4 B	3 E	5 C

PAGE 146: Spot (It!)
the Difference

PAGE 146: Wobble

While several squares have been swapped around, one depicts a section of the Rooster, instead of the Alligator.

PAGE 147: Find the Pair
The Snowflake.

Scribble notes

Scribble notes

Scribble notes

Scribble notes

Scribble notes

Scribble notes

Spot It! sets used in this book

1 2 3

0 **Blue Zero** 1 **Red One** 2 **Orange Two** 3 **Green Three** 4 **Purple Four** 5 **Yellow Five** 6 **Purple Six** 7 **Blue Seven** 8 **Red Eight** 9 **Yellow Nine**

 Purple Square   **Green Circle** **Red Rectangle**   **Yellow Triangle** 0 **Purple Zero**   **Blue One** 2 **Red Two** 3 **Orange Three** 4 **Green Four** 5 **Purple Five**

6 **Yellow Six** 7 **Red Seven** 8 **Orange Eight** 9 **Green Nine**   **Green Square**   **Orange Circle**   **Yellow Circle**   **Pruple Rectangle**   **Orange Rectangle** **Blue Triangle**

 Red Triangle

Animals

Sea lion	Rabbit	Mouse	Jellyfish	Octopus
Snake	Starfish	Shark	Fish	Tiger
Lion	Owl	Pelican	Blue bird	Raccoon
Spider	Polar bear	Squirrel	Sloth	Kangaroo
Panda	Penguin	Wolf	Zebra	Koala
Snail	Frog	Hippopotamus	Sheep	Horse
Mosquito	Whale	Scorpion	Seahorse	Turtle
Deer	Aligator	Crab	Dog	Camel
Goat	Cow	Gorilla	Flamingo	Beaver
Donkey	Hedgehog	Cock	Eagle	Cat
Parrot	Brown bear	Buffalo	Dolphin	Duck
Grasshopper	Bat			

Spot It! sets used in this book

 Light bulb
 Anchor
 Spider
 Tree
 Baby Bottle
 Bomb
 Snowman
 Gingerbread Man
 Mouth/Lips
 Candle

 Cactus
 Lock
 Carrot
 Knight/Horse
 Cat
 Dog
 Target
 Scissors
 Key
 Music/Treble Clef

 Clown
 Ladybug
 Heart
 Pencil
 Dolphin
 Dinosaur/T-Rex
 Dobbly
 Dragon
 Lightning
 Ghost

 Fire
 Maple Leaf
 Daisy
 Snowflake
 Cheese
 Ice Cube
 Water/Drop
 Clock
 Igloo
 Moon

 Turtle/Tortoise
 Glasses
 Hammer
 Eye
 Bird
 Four-Leaf Clover
 Stop Sign
 Exclamation Mark
 Question Mark
 Apple

 Sun
 Paint
 Skull and Crossbones
 Spider's Web
 Car
 Yin and Yang
 Zebra

Kids

Cat	Tiger	Rooster	Bear	Crab	Gorilla	Zebra	Ladybug, ladybird	Lion	Owl
Duck	Horse	Whale	Camel	Penguin	Tortoise, turtle	Octopus	Crocodile, alligator	Parrot	Sheep
Cow	Kangaroo	Frog, toad	Hippopotamus	Fish	Elephant	Dolphin	Shark	Snake	Rabbit

Dog

Spot It! sets used in this book

Waterproof

Surfboard	Bucket	Kite	Swimfin/Flipper	Rudder	Pebbles/Rocks	Cocktail	Shovel	Camera	Sun Hat
Palmtree	Blowfish	Splash/Spotlt	Lei/Garland	Frisbee	Ball	Footprint	Icebox	Bathing Suit	Orca
Sunglasses	Sand Castle	Seahorse	Conch Shell	Wave	Calamar	Watermelon	Scuba Mask	Flip Flop	Sailing Ship
Anchor	Ice Lolly	Urchin	Water Pistol	Lighthouse	Fishing rod	Life Buoy	Coral	Deckchair	Mermaid
Pelican	Bubbles	Oyster	Arm buoy	Hammock	Suncream	Aloha	Beach Towel	Torch	Parasol
Crab	Shark	Sun	Tennis racket	Coconut	Book	Jellyfish			